Hi, Mom

mom

dad

grandma

grandpa

sister

brother

teacher

puppy

Hi, Mom.

Hi.

Hi, Dad.

Hi.

Hi, Grandma.

Hi.

Hi, Grandpa.

Hi.

Hi, Teacher.

Hi.

Hi, Puppy.

Woof.

Let's learn about
the United States of America (USA).

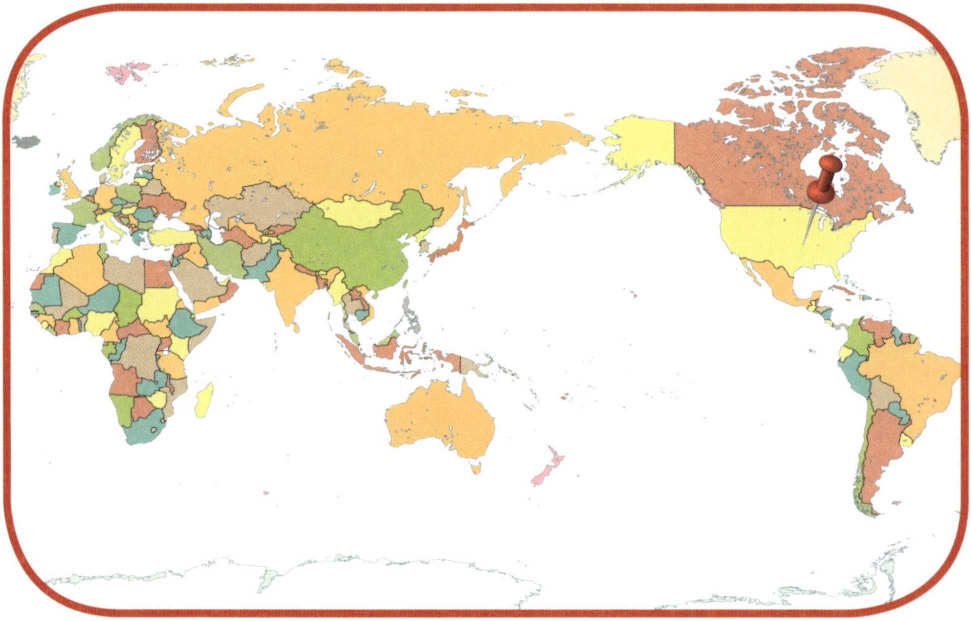

Flag of USA
(The Star-Spangled Banner)

Statue of Liberty